MW00625768

Taking Every Thought Captive

Spiritual Workouts
to Help Renew Your
Mind in God's Truth

by Alaine Pakkala

©1995 by Alaine Pakkala
Printed in the United States of America.

Cover design and page layout by Chad Planner

Scripture taken from the NEW AMERICAN STANDARD BIBLE.
©1960, 1962, 1963, 1968, 1971, 1972, 1973, 1975, 1977 by The
Lockman Foundation. Used by permission.

Publisher's Cataloging in Publication
Pakkala, Alaine.
    Taking every thought captive : spiritual workouts to help renew
your mind in God's truth / Alaine Pakkala.—1st ed.
    p. cm.
    Preassigned LCCN: 94-096711.
    ISBN 1-886461-32-5

    1. Meditation—Christianity. 2. Spiritual exercises. 3. Bible—
Study and teaching. 4. Spiritual life—Christianity.   I. Title
BV4813.P35 1995   248.34
                                   QBI94—21174

 Lydia Press

Outline of Topics Covered

"Getting To Know The Father" Bible Study

"I Will Sing To The Lord" Meditation Book

> *"For though we walk in the flesh we do
> not war according to the flesh, for the
> weapons of our warfare are not of the
> flesh, but are divinely powerful for the
> destruction of fortresses. We are destroy-
> ing speculations and every lofty thing
> raised up against the knowledge of
> God, and we are taking every thought
> captive to the obedience of Christ."*
> *(2 Cor. 10:3-5)*

This training guide answers the questions: How can I take charge of what goes through my mind? How can I resist the enemy? How can I see old patterns in my life replaced with new ones?

These thirty-minute "workouts" may be used by any-one who realizes the need to take charge of what they allow to pass through their minds. It is especially designed to help survivors of abuse activate their wills and renew their minds in the truth of God.

It may be best used in a one-on-one training session with another Christian to help keep things on track, although it may be done alone as well.

The word of God tells us to "have the high praises of God in your mouths and a two-edged sword in your hand." (Ps. 149:6) With this in mind, each workout is divided into two major sections: "Drawing Near To God" and "Resisting the Enemy". There are also suggestions for daily practice habits to follow up after each weekly workout session.

For too long, many of us have been harassed, confused or defeated by our thoughts. The goal of this training manual is to begin to put a stop to that as we actively agree with God's plan to renew our minds through the Truth.

Prayer of confession before beginning:

> *"Heavenly Father, I confess that I have allowed my mind to be controlled and to control me, instead of me controlling my mind. I take back any ground I may have given by doing this in the past. I destroy any hindrances or patterns of thought that are based on my past consent. I choose to aggressively take every thought captive to the obedience of Christ. Help me, Lord, as I begin this study. May You be glorified as I become more and more like Christ. In the name of my Lord and Savior, Jesus Christ, AMEN."*

Workout #1

Drawing Near To God

Why Do This Workout?

All Christians are told to exercise control over their minds. Scripture paints a clear picture of the warfare we are all engaged in—a struggle between living a life consistent with the truth of who we are in Christ, or living a life based on subtle (and not so subtle) lies and deceptions.

Scripture also pinpoints the battlefield. Like a general tapping his pointer on a map in the war room, God's Word zeros in on the site of the heated battles, both big and small. The battlefield is the mind (2 Cor. 4:4; 11:3). These battles determine how we live out each day. Our thoughts are the starting points for our actions as well as our reactions.

Is it any wonder then, that our enemy Satan hurls his well-placed darts not generally at our physical body, or at some external focus. He sends them to the control center of our life—our mind. Thoughts: fleeting thoughts, well-entrenched thoughts, enticing thoughts, harassing thoughts, accusing thoughts, vague thoughts, confusing thoughts, bizarre thoughts, distracting thoughts, lustful thoughts, condemning thoughts.

But God is at work too. Through His Holy Spirit, He plants thoughts in our minds also—truths from His Word. Good thoughts, uplifting thoughts, comforting thoughts, strengthening thoughts, convicting thoughts, life-giving thoughts, encouraging thoughts.

Also, from the moment we are saved (transferred out of Satan's kingdom, and brought into God's kingdom) the Lord, through His Holy Spirit, begins a process of renewing or repatterning our mind, changing the way we think (Col. 3:9 & 10; 2 Cor. 4:16).We have the bold promise in Romans 12:1 & 2 that as our mind is renewed, our life will be transformed (like our word "metamorphosized"). Similar to how a caterpillar amazingly becomes a beautiful butterfly, our lives too take on a completely new form.

The change isn't simply an outward, cosmetic "getting our act together". Instead, the picture we are given by Paul in Romans is one of a drastic, deep, inward change that is reflected in how we act outwardly.

What causes this change? The agent is the Holy Spirit and the tool is the truth found in God's Word—the truth about us, about God, about others. God tells us He desires truth "in the innermost being" (Ps. 51:6), the very core of our lives. All of us however, to one degree or another, have misconceptions, distortions or lies that control our feelings and actions.

How do we dislodge them? What is our part in this renewal process? We are told to "gird your minds for action" (1 Peter 1:13) and to "bring every thought captive" (2 Cor. 10:5). How, practically, do we do that? Quite simply, by practicing it.

Too long many of us have allowed our thoughts to come and go, to run unchecked through our minds. We need to first see where the lies are and then replace them with the truth. We CAN and NEED to take charge!

Those who have, by God's power and grace, survived severe abuse, also have another factor to consider. The numbing power of overwhelming violence against them has silenced their will to resist. The feelings of helplessness, powerlessness and vulnerability they have experienced over and over again, shuts down something inside of them, something God now wants to revive. Like a muscle that has atrophied because of lack of use, their will needs to begin to be exercised in agreement with God's truth.

To sum up:
- The mind is the battlefield.
- I need a renewed mind.
- My mind is renewed by the truth.
- My part in the renewing is to know and act on the basis of the truth.
- My will needs to be reactivated.

Exalting God Through His Word

One of the best ways to begin renewing your mind, is to fill it with Scripture verses that lift up or focus on the Lord. Reading His Word back to God is an excellent way to exalt Him. Copy the following verses on 3x5 cards and read them aloud.

> Rev. 5:12 & 13
> Ps. 113:1-3
> Ps. 34:1-3

Before you say the verses, read this statement aloud:

> "*I choose to exalt Christ who is my Lord and my God through these verses of praise. I bind anything that would hinder me from reading, hearing, remembering, or believing them. I activate my will in agreement with these truths.*"

Resisting The Enemy

Besides drawing near to God, we also need to resist the enemy. Read aloud the Daily Commitment Prayer that follows:

Daily Commitment Prayer

Father, I come to You in the name of the Lord Jesus Christ. I claim the blood of the Lord Jesus as my protection during this time of prayer. I address only the True and Living God. I refuse any involvement of Satan in my prayers.

In the name of Jesus Christ, I command Satan to leave my presence with all his wicked spirits and I bring the blood of the Lord Jesus between us.

Father, I ask that You help me during this time of prayer. I thank You that the weapons of my warfare are not carnal, human or fleshly but are mighty through God to the pulling down of strongholds, imaginations, and every high thing that exalts itself against the knowledge and experience of God and brings every thought into obedience to Christ.

In the name of the Lord Jesus Christ, I resist and cancel every plan, I smash and break every stronghold that has been formed against me and my priesthood. I bind Satan's work in this area and loose his hold upon my priesthood. I submit my priesthood to You, dear Lord.

I take authority over all wicked spirits in and around the house that have been assigned to hinder me and my priesthood today. I bind you in the name of the Lord Jesus Christ. I command all wicked spirits in the house to leave and I bind you outside the house. I submit those bonds to You, heavenly Father.

I resist and cancel every plan, I smash and break every stronghold against me for this day. I bind and destroy all the enemy's work against my mind, my emotions, my will, my body, my nerves, my spirit and its functions, and against the work of the Holy Spirit in my life. I resist all counterfeits, hindrances to my ministry and calling, my spiritual gifts, my prayers, and my authority in Christ.

Father, I thank and praise You for Your salvation and deliverance so rich and free. I praise You that while I was yet a sinner, Christ died for me and ransomed me from the fall. I now claim the blood and righteousness of Christ as my only hope for salvation. I thank You that I was justified, sanctified, given eternal life, and made an heir of God and a co-heir with Christ. I claim all the blessings that are mine because of it.

I claim my union in the crucifixion where I was placed in Christ and as He died for sin, I died to sin. I put off the dead old nature with all its deceitful lusts. I reckon myself now dead indeed to sin.

I claim my union in Christ in the resurrection where I was raised to new life and I put on the new man created in righteousness and true holiness and claim the resurrection power in my life.

I thank You for my union in Christ in the glorification where Jesus was seated at the right hand of God the Father. You have placed me there in Christ. I claim my place there where all principalities, powers, and wicked spirits are put under the feet of Jesus and thus under me. I therefore declare that all principalities, powers, and wicked spirits are subject to me because of this.

I thank You for my union in Christ in Pentecost where I was baptized by the Holy Spirit. I claim the filling of the Blessed Holy Spirit, all His ministry, and His fruit in my life for this day.

I thank You for my union in Christ in the promises; that in Jesus they are all yea and amen. I claim my place as an adult son by the adoption of the Spirit where I now have all the inheritance and authority as an heir of God and co-heir with Jesus Christ. I claim _____ (any promises God has given you personally as well as Phil 4:19; John 7:38; Eph. 1:3; etc).

I reject and resist all the endeavors of Satan and his wicked spirits to rob me of the full will of God. I claim God's full will for me. I surrender myself to You, Lord, as a living sacrifice. I chose not to be conformed to this world but transformed by the renewing of my mind so that I may know the full and complete will of God in experience. If the enemy has any ground or hold in my life that robs me of God's will, I pray You will push it out and expose it that I may be totally Yours. I refuse to believe my feelings but place my faith completely in You for victory.

I thank You for Your full provision for victory. I put on the full armor of God: the breastplate of righteousness, the girdle of truth, the sandals of peace on my feet, the helmet of salvation on my head, the sword of the Spirit in my hand, and I cover myself from head to foot with the shield of faith.

I claim all the victory the Lord Jesus Christ has provided for me where He made a show of principalities, powers and wicked spirits, leading them in a victory procession, triumphing over them by His cross. I reject them out of my life, all their insinuations, accusations, condemnations and temptations, hindering, lying, counterfeiting and distorting of the truth. Keep me aggressive in prayer mentally, physically, and spiritually to withstand the enemy in all things.

I choose to please You, Lord, in all things, to obey Your Word, and to live in harmony with You. I choose all the work of the Lord Jesus Christ in my life—His crucifixion, resurrection, and glorification, and all the work of Pentecost (the ministry, fruit and filling of the Holy Spirit). I refuse to be discouraged. You're the God of all hope. I surrender myself to You completely.

I resist and reject every endeavor of Satan to rob me of the full will of God. I claim God's will. I now resist and reject all the forces of Satan that are active in my life today. I do all this in the name of the Lord Jesus Christ. AMEN.

Daily Practice Habits

1) Pray the "Daily Commitment Prayer" aloud every morning.

2) Read aloud the "Drawing Near" verses at least twice a day (perhaps morning and evening). Check off the days you do these "habits".

This Week's Spiritual Re-conditioning Record

____ Day 1   ____ Day 2   ____ Day 3   ____ Day 4

____ Day 5   ____ Day 6   ____ Day 7

Drawing Near To God

Our Authority in Christ

You have authority over the enemy because of your union with Jesus Christ. As a Christian, you are now "in Christ". This means, among other things, that He has made you an heir of God and a co-heir with Jesus Christ. Because God is greater than Satan and you are now in Christ, you can use the authority He has given you to resist Satan (Luke 10:18 & 19).

You can never stand up under your own power against the enemy. It must be according to His power that works in you. The Bible keeps reminding us that God is the one who has won the victory (1 Cor. 15:57; Deut. 3:22). To-day's verses focus on the truth that we have authority in Christ and that He is the one who has overcome the enemy. Your job is to agree with the truth that Christ is victor!

1) Look up these verses and write them on 3x5 cards for use this week.

    Deut. 3:22
    Ps. 108:13
    1 John 4:4
    1 Cor. 15:57

2) Pray this prayer for understanding:

> *"Lord, I don't understand much about my union with Christ. Please help me to realize more of what it means. Teach me to rely on You and not on my own self-effort to defeat Satan in my life. Show me the difference between the two. In the name of Jesus Christ, Amen."*

Resisting The Enemy

Using Our Authority to "Forbid"

What you say is very powerful. Sometimes controlling your mouth is the first step to controlling your thoughts. Saying things aloud is a good way of avoiding the confusion that can fill your mind. One of the things you can do is to use the word "forbid" as you command the enemy to leave you alone. You might say "I forbid the enemy to cause me any bodily harm today." Or "I forbid the enemy to bother me while I am at church today."

Remember, you have authority over him in Christ. Don't be blackmailed by fear. Satan may give you the thought: "If you do this (or that) it will REALLY get bad for you." Don't let him intimidate you. Satan is a bluffer. You have authority over him in Christ. Simply forbid him to retaliate or intimidate you. The enemy never gives up without a fight, but **HE ALWAYS GIVES UP!!!**

Using Positive Affirmations—"This I Know..." Lists

Saying things that are true, even if you don't feel or "believe" them is a very good weapon to use against the lies that control you. Remember: it is not being hypocritical to say the truth and "choose" to believe it even when your thoughts are saying something different than your mouth. You are simply affirming the truth.

These "positive affirmations" can help you when you feel yourself being overwhelmed by fear, depression or confusion. At times like that, it is especially important that you focus on things that are true. It may be helpful before those times come to write out what I call my "This I know..." list of truths. The title comes from the Bible verse that says "cease striving (let go, relax) and know that I am God" (Ps. 46:10), and is a way of resisting the flood of lying feelings and thoughts inside.

For example, if you feel that the pressures of your circumstances are about to drive you crazy, your thoughts are probably telling you lies like: "God doesn't care what happens to me"; "There is no hope"; "The enemy's work is too strong"; etc.

Your "This I know..." list would be based on what the Bible says is true for you. It might read: "God is on my side"; "There is hope because I belong to the God of Hope"; "No one is stronger than my God."

Make your "This I know..." list about your situation. (Use the list on page 17). Make the sentences basic truths that the Bible says about you, about God or about others. Perhaps someone else can help you discover what to write.

One of the ways to decide what truths you need to affirm is to think through what sentences usually are in your mind when you get into a certain situation. Just write down the opposite of these negative statements. When you have your list, read it aloud. (If you are not able as yet to say things like this aloud, say them inside as loudly as you can, and keep trying to say them aloud too. You will eventually be able to do it.)

Daily Practice Habits

1. Continue to read aloud the "Daily Commitment Prayer" every morning.

2. Read aloud the "Drawing Near to God" verses from this week's workout at least twice a day.

3. Read aloud your "This I know..." list every day.

This Week's Spiritual Re-conditioning Record

___ Day 1   ___ Day 2   ___ Day 3   ___ Day 4

___ Day 5   ___ Day 6   ___ Day 7

The TRUTH is that:

    1)

    2)

    3)

    4)

    5)

    6)

    7)

    8)

    9)

    10)

Drawing Near To God

Steeping Your Mind in the Word

You cannot be prepared to resist the enemy unless you spend time in the Word of God. The Bible calls it the Sword of the Spirit (Eph. 6:17). We are told that the truth of the Word will replace lying feelings in our soul as we allow it to soak into our lives (Heb. 4:12).

The main purpose of saturating your mind in the truth is, first of all, because it leads you to worship the God who wrote it. God will not love you more if you have a regular "Quiet Time", but you will love God more as you understand what He is like and what He has done for you.

Secondly, it gives you the spiritual nourishment you need to grow in the truth. (See the end of this workout for a list of suggestions on how to start or rekindle a daily time with God.)

How to Begin Meditating on the Word

One of the things you need to learn how to do is to meditate on God's Word. Unlike the New-Age style mystic meditation (with its goal of an empty mind), Christian meditation involves "setting your mind", using it to focus in on God's perspective. It is taking time to let His truth take root in your mind. When you meditate on the Truth, you know God better and see yourself more accurately.

One of the reasons we sometimes don't get much out of Scripture is that we read through it too fast. Practice meditating by taking one verse and forcing yourself to **READ SLOWLY** through it. As you read, check your mind for **COMPREHENSION**. In other words, ask yourself "What is it saying? What is being described in this verse?"

Another good tool to use while meditating is to **SUMMARIZE** what you have just read before going on to the next sentence or verse. This is taking what you have read and putting it in your own words.

One of the main hindrances to meditating on God's Word is our inability to **CONCENTRATE**. Lack of concentration can be overcome in two ways: First, you need to forbid the enemy to interfere with your meditation. Satan will oppose you by flooding your mind with distracting thoughts whenever you try to concentrate on the Word. As you resist him by continually focusing your mind back on the verse, it will eventually become easier and easier to concentrate.

For those who hear "voices" or comments constantly being made inside as you read the Word, there is an additional suggestion. Don't get caught up in arguing with or listening to the voices. They are not from God. Simply forbid the enemy to interfere with your meditation and ask God to deal with the source of the voices. Then, if and when they come back, ignore them. Eventually they'll stop.

Secondly, your concentration can be improved by one simple thing: **PRACTICE**. Especially if you have allowed your mind to wander in the past, or have a habit of day-dreaming, you may find it extra difficult to concentrate. Keep practicing. Eventually you will be able to stay focused as you meditate on Scripture. Part of the meaning in the original Greek language for the word we translate "meditate" is to "take pains with". Learning to meditate is work. But the payoff in terms of spiritual growth and joyful freedom makes it very much worth your efforts.

Another tool to help you meditate on truth is to **MEMORIZE** Scripture. A lot could be said about this topic, but we will only touch on it briefly. Here are some suggestions to help you begin to memorize the Word:

- Resist the enemy's attempt to hinder you by forbidding him to interfere.

- Refuse all lies such as: "I can't memorize"; "I don't have time to memorize"; etc.. I know a lady who "wasn't good at memorizing", who spent just fifteen minutes a day working at it. At the end of 20 years, with only that small amount of daily time, she had the entire New Testament memorized! It can be done, even if you "don't have a mind that remembers things easily".

- Ask God to give you a desire to memorize the Word. Pray like David did in Psalm 119 where he asks God to help him in his attitude about God's Word.

- Don't allow Satan to discourage you by pointing out your past failures in this area. Persevere. You WILL succeed!

- Start small. Plan to memorize one verse each month or several a month.

- Choose "ammo" verses. Begin with verses that relate to a stronghold (or a weak area) in your life. For example, if you have trouble with lust, begin memorizing verses about holiness, purity, etc. This type of ammunition can be of special use during the night as fears and troubling thoughts flood over you. If the verses have been memorized, they can become weapons against the lying feelings and the harassing, distorted thoughts.

- Learn how to "pray through" verses of Scripture. This is like praying them back to God, asking Him for understanding and affirming that you believe what He says. Take, for example, Psalm 124:

> " *'Had it not been the Lord who was on our side' let Israel now say, 'had it not been the Lord who was on our side,*

when men rose up against us; Then they would have swallowed us alive, when their anger was kindled against us.'"

You might mediate on this Psalm by praying something like:

"Thank You Lord, that You are on my side. Thank You that even when things oppose me, You are there and are preventing me from being 'swallowed'! You are so strong. No one is stronger than You. I choose to be on Your side too. Help me stay close to You."

It's best when you are praying through parts of Scripture to choose only a few verses. Take your time. Spending time like this in His presence is wonderful!! But it takes practice to develop this skill. So don't give up before it becomes a habit.

1. Use the meditation tools mentioned above—reading slowly, questioning for comprehension, summarizing, practicing concentration and praying through Scripture on one or more of the following verses:

   Ps. 37:23 & 24
   John 16:33
   Rom. 8:38 & 39
   Col. 1:13
   Ps. 32:7

2. Copy down several of these verses for use this week.

Taking Back the Night

Often nighttime is a difficult time for some. One way to help get a good night's sleep is to fill your mind with Scripture just as you're going to bed. You also can forbid the enemy to bother you at night. Once he sees that you will continue to take authority over him about this, he will give up in this area of harassment.

Later in this workout, you will find a list of "Verses to Meditate on Before Going to Bed" as well as a "Prayer for Restful Sleep". Read through these two and remember: there is nothing magical about the prayer. It is simply an affirmation of what you as a Christian have chosen for your night.

Also, many people find that they have vivid, intense dreams that they can't seem to shake out of their head after they wake up. It may help to affirm the following:

> "*I disavow any dreams that came from Satan or any that are being used by him to torment me. In the name of Jesus Christ, I refuse· everything that happened in my conscious mind or in the 'deep' last night that did not come by way of the cross of the Lord Jesus Christ.*"

Daily Practice Habits

1. Meditate on one or more of the verses you have copied from the "Drawing Near to God" section each day.

2. Continue to read aloud the "Daily Commitment Prayer" each day.

3. Read over the "Verses to Meditate on Before Going to Bed" and pray through the "Prayer for Restful Sleep" each night.

This Week's Spiritual Re-conditioning Record

___ Day 1   ___ Day 2   ___ Day 3   ___ Day 4

___ Day 5   ___ Day 6   ___ Day 7

Verses to Meditate on Before Going to Bed

"*In* peace I will both lie down and sleep, for Thou alone, O Lord, dost make me to dwell in safety."

(Ps. 4:8)

"*When* *I* lie down, *I* will not be afraid. When *I* lie down, *my* sleep will be sweet. *I* will not be afraid of sudden fear, nor of the onslaught of the wicked when it comes; For the Lord will be *my* confidence and will keep *my* foot from being caught."

(Prov. 3:24-6, personalized)

"The fear of (reverence for) the Lord leads to life, so that one may sleep satisfied, untouched by evil."

(Prov. 19:23)

"*I* lay down and slept; I awoke, for the Lord sustains me. I will not be afraid of ten thousands of people who have set themselves against me round about."

(Ps. 3:5 & 6)

"*When* I remember Thee on my bed, I meditate on Thee in the night watches. For Thou hast been my help, and in the shadow of Thy wings I sing for joy. My soul clings to Thee; Thy right hand upholds me."

(Ps. 63:6-8)

"*My* help comes from the Lord, who made heaven and earth. He will not allow *my* foot to slip; He who keeps *me* will not slumber. Behold, He who keeps Israel will neither slumber nor sleep."

(Ps. 121:2-4, personalized)

"*He* who dwells in the shelter of the Most High will abide in the shadow of the Almighty. I will say to the Lord, "My refuge and my fortress, My God in whom I trust!" For it is He who delivers *me* from the snare of the trapper, and from the deadly pestilence. He will cover *me* with His pinions, and under His wings *I* may seek refuge. His faithfulness is a shield and bulwark. *I* will not be afraid of the terror by night, or of the arrow that flies by day; Of the pestilence that stalks in darkness, or of the destruction that lays waste at noon. A thousand may fall at *my* side, and ten thousand at *my* right hand; But it shall not approach *me*. *I* will only look on with *my* eyes, and see the recompense of the wicked. For *I* have made the Lord, *my* refuge, even the Most High, *my* dwelling place. No evil will befall *me*, nor will any plague come near *my* tent. For He will give His angels charge concerning *me*, to guard *me* in all *my* ways."

(Ps. 91:1-11, personalized)

Prayer for Restful Sleep

> "*Heavenly Father, I come to You and put my sleep for this night into Your hands. I refuse any thoughts, dreams or sleep patterns that are not from the True and Living God. I cancel any plans Satan may have for this night and replace them with God's plans for my sleep.*

26

I refuse all fears, dreams, nightmares, insomnia, restlessness, anxiety, mental pictures or racing thoughts. I take authority over any wicked spirits who have been assigned to hinder me tonight. I bind them in the name of the Lord Jesus Christ, and submit these bonds to the Holy Spirit of the True and Living God.

I take authority over all wicked spirits in or around my house and I bind them outside the house. I put on the whole armor of God and choose to resist Satan. I claim the promise of God that as I resist Satan, he must flee.

Heavenly Father, protect me, comfort me, be close to me. Give me a restful night of sleep this night. I praise You, Lord Jesus. I exalt You. I acknowledge my allegiance to You this night. I pray all these things in the powerful name of Your Son, Jesus Christ. Amen. "

Suggestions on How to Start/Rekindle Your "Quiet Time" with God

1. Resist the lie that time with God is optional.

2. Realize the resistance from Satan. Forbid the enemy to interfere.

3. Remember God desires your fellowship.

4. Focus on the reasons for doing it: to worship God and to get food for your spiritual growth.

5. Make time—prepare the night before by making choices so you will be awake and alert in the morning.

6. Resist the "rabbit's foot" mentally (don't become devoted to the habit but to the One you're meeting with).

7. Resist the lie that it gives you brownie points with God or that He will love you more if you spend time with Him.

8. Take your time. Set an unhurried pace.

9. Have a plan. Don't use the unorganized "Bible roulette" style of reading wherever the Bible falls open to.

10. Don't do all the talking.

11. Avoid self-reliance. Without God's help, you can't maintain a vital time with Him each day. Ask God for His help and guidance.

12. Aim at quality, not quantity. Seven minutes is a good beginning place. Plan for success by setting reachable goals.

13. Be flexible. Avoid ruts.

14. Avoid the "academic", checklist approach in which you focus on just getting it done, not on trying to get anything out of it.

15. After reading, summarize what you've read. Ask yourself: "What does this show me about God?" or "What can I try to do differently today based on what I have just read?"

16. Persevere in capturing wandering thoughts.

17. If you're too busy, decide what you will need to leave out so that you can have time to meet with the Lord every day.

18. Resist discouragement. Keep trying!!!

Workout #4

Drawing Near To God

Worshipping the King of Kings

A renewed mind is a mind that is so filled with the right things (truth) that little room is left for the wrong things (lies). One of the best ways to agree with God's truth is to use His Word as you spend time worshipping Him. Real worship is going beyond just thanking Him for things, to focusing in on who He is and what He is like.

You may find the "I Will Sing to the Lord" booklet included in this training guide (pp.83-112) helpful as a focus point for your worship. It includes sections on worshipping Him by: Exalting Him from His Word; Confessing His Name; Meditating on What Our God is Like; Focusing on the Cross; Meditating on the Incomparable Christ; and Looking Forward to His Return.

Write out the following verses and read them aloud.

> Rev. 4:8
> Rev. 5:9 & 10
> 1 Tim. 1:17
> 1 Tim. 6:15 & 16

"Is This Thought from God?"

We know that Satan is called the deceiver and that he sometimes disguises himself as an "angel of light". It is safe to assume then, that he will try to trick you with lying thoughts, feelings or "spiritual" experiences. How do you know if they are from God or if the enemy is tricking you? There are several safeguards which I will mention in a minute. But first, let's put down some basics.

To begin with, the Lord will never tell you something or give you a particular feeling or experience that goes the opposite direction from what He has already put down in the Bible. What if you get a thought that says, "I should hurt myself as a punishment for how bad I am"? Well, as you have been steeping your mind in the Word of God, you remember that IT says that you are precious in God's sight. You are forgiven by your Heavenly Father for the sins you commit. You should "nourish and cherish" your body. So you can tell immediately that the Lord would NEVER give you that kind of a thought.

Let's take some other examples. Maybe you are in church when suddenly you get so sleepy that you can hardly keep your eyes open, even though you are very interested in what the Pastor is saying. Is this just a natural tiredness or is it the enemy making you sleepy? Or if you have a "spiritual" experience that leaves you feeling all tingly, is that from God, or could it be from someone else? How do you know?

For one thing, we need to remember that Satan is not a creator, but he is a counterfeiter. That means that he can give us something that is not the real thing and try to get us to accept it as the genuine article. We are told in God's Word not to be ignorant of his devices. We are also warned to test our experiences to see if they are from God (1 John 4:1-3).

Also, God forbids us as Christians to mess with psychic powers (Deut. 18:9-14). If you have had psychic powers or experiences in the past, you need to be sure that you are not using these powers or seeking the feeling that these abilities bring. Psychic powers are real, but they are never from or used by God.

We are also warned by God not to seek supernatural experiences. In Matt. 12:38-40, Christ says that it is agreeing with an evil generation when you crave signs and wonders apart from the truth of the Word.

Many people have been trapped and sucked deeper and deeper into deception by believing the lie that all that is supernatural must be from God. Satan can give an overwhelming sense of peace, joy, knowledge of the future, false gifts of tongues, bodily sensations like tingling and many other seemingly "spiritual" experiences.

Should I be scared then? No, not at all. It's best to be cautious but not afraid. Here are some safeguards against deception that I have found helpful:

- Saturate your mind in the Word of God so you can detect counterfeits and lies. (For example, learn the guidelines the Bible gives for the proper use of spiritual gifts so you will know when they are being used in an unscriptural way.)

- Keep your wits about you! Double-check any experience that seems out of your control or that by-passes the mind. God does His work through a renewed mind, not around it.

- Deal with any known sin. Sin in one area that you refuse to deal with can make you more susceptible to deception in another area.

- Realize that God is faithful and that the Holy Spirit will detect deception if we allow Him to. The Bible speaks of those who are maturing "who because of practice, have their senses trained to discern good and evil."
(Heb. 5:14)

Using the "If" Prayer

One of the safest things is to be willing to put a thought, feeling or experience in neutral if you are not sure whether it is from God or not. One of the most helpful affirmations you can make when you aren't sure is: "If this is from the True and Living God, I accept it. If it is not, I reject it. Show me, Lord, if it is from You." As you continue to make this affirmation, you will become more and more convinced about who the thought or feeling or "spiritual" experience is from. (Remember that in addition to Satan, our flesh can also give us feelings or experiences. Sometimes we make the mistake of believing that these are from God.)

Daily Practice Habits

1. Meditate daily on the verses from this week's "Drawing Near to God" section.

2. Continue to read aloud the "Daily Commitment Prayer".

3. Pray daily:

   "Lord, I ask You to uncover any thoughts, feelings or experiences that I have had that are not from You. Help me to be on the alert to the enemy's counterfeits and deceptions. Today I choose only truth in every area of my life. I pray in the name of Jesus Christ my Lord. Amen."

4. Continue using the "Verses for Meditation Before Going to Bed" and the "Prayer for Restful Sleep" each night.

This Week's Spiritual Re-conditioning Record

____ Day 1   ____ Day 2   ____ Day 3   ____ Day 4

____ Day 5   ____ Day 6   ____ Day 7

Drawing Near To God

The Weapon of Praise

The truth of God is a powerful weapon against the lies and tricks of the enemy. That's why it is so crucial to steep your mind in God's Word.

But praise is a weapon too. In it, we affirm the truths about who God is and what He is like. Sometimes the only way to dislodge a mental fog, a cloud of depression or an uncontrollable flood of vile thoughts is to use the weapon of praise.

Usually, when we need to praise the Lord the most, we feel the least like doing it. Ask the Lord ahead of time, when you're doing fairly well, to remind you to take up the weapon of praise when you need to. Then when He reminds you, do it.

If you can't get started by yourself, sometimes playing a praise album helps unlock the praises the Holy Spirit inside of you is bringing to your mind. Have one ready to go on the days you wake up and realize that it could be a bad day.

Also, as we've mentioned before, it's important to

memorize verses that praise God so you will have them beside you when you need some "ammo".

Resisting The Enemy

Refusing and Choosing

You have authority in Christ. One of the ways to exercise that authority is by making "Refuse" and "Choose" statements. By them, you are announcing that you refuse the enemy's ways and choose God's ways. You are refusing the lying feelings inside (for example, the feeling that God doesn't love you) and choosing the feelings that line up with the truth (that God considers you His "special treasure" Ex. 19:5, margin; Deut. 7;6, margin; and "the apple of His eye" Zech. 2:8; Ps. 17:8).

When you read or hear things that are true, instead of saying "I can't believe that!" say "That's true and I choose to believe it." Remember: don't wait for your feelings to change first. Change your mouth and then your mind and finally your feelings will be changed too!

There is great power in what you say aloud, or affirm as true. Many times when you silently agree with the truth, your affirmations seem to somehow get locked up inside. The best thing to do is to say your refuse/choose affirmations aloud. These "spiritual announcements" of choosing the truth help to strengthen you and they also help to resist Satan and his lies.

There are many things you can refuse/choose that need to be announced:

- I refuse all the enemy's lies and choose only the truth of God for today.

- I refuse all discouragement and choose to hope in the God of all hope.

- I refuse to allow my mind to wander when I am trying to read the Word.

- I choose to concentrate.

- I forbid the enemy to interfere. I refuse all fear and choose the peace that goes beyond all understanding. I refuse to be intimidated by the enemy.

- I choose to trust in God's protection. I refuse all despair, suicidal thoughts and depression.

- I choose to be filled with the hope and joy of the Lord today.

1) Read Psalm. 63:1-8 and make an "I refuse...I choose" list of statements based on what it says in these verses. (For example, "I *refuse* a coldness towards God. I *choose* to long after knowing Him better.")

2) Make an "I refuse...I choose" statement about each of these verses from Psalm 119:

       verse 27

       verse 29

       verses 33-40

Daily Practice Habits

1) This week, continue to pray the "Daily Commitment Prayer" and "Prayer for Restful Sleep" each day.

2) Copy down on 3x5 cards several of the verses from the "Drawing Near to God" section from this workout, and meditate on them this week.

3) Look for ways to use your "I refuse...I choose" affirmations this week.

This Week's Spiritual Re-conditioning Record

___ Day 1   ___ Day 2   ___ Day 3   ___ Day 4

___ Day 5   ___ Day 6   ___ Day 7

Workout #6

Drawing Near to God

Replacing Distortions About God with the Truth

Many times our view of God is distorted. This is especially true if the person the Lord intended to be a picture of what the Heavenly Father is like (our earthly father) did not accurately portray Him. Sometimes if there are problems trusting God it is due, in part, to the fact that the person has a distorted view of the God he is trying to trust. Often, what you believe about what God is like is shown in your prayers, or how you approach Him. (For additional studies in what God is like, see the "Getting to Know the Father" Bible Study which begins on page 49.

Read aloud the following list of true facts about God and what He thinks about you. Before each statement say "I choose to believe that...".

GOD WANTS TO HAVE AN INTIMATE RELATION-SHIP WITH ME

GOD KNOWS EVERYTHING ABOUT ME AND HE STILL LOVES ME

GOD'S LOVE FOR ME IS NOT INFLUENCED BY ANYTHING I EVER DID OR WILL DO

THE CREATOR OF THE UNIVERSE LOVES ME

GOD IS IN CONTROL OF EVERYTHING IN MY LIFE

GOD NEVER MAKES A MISTAKE

GOD UNDERSTANDS FULLY EVEN WHEN NO ONE ELSE DOES

GOD HAS A PLAN FOR THE CROOKED PLACES

Resisting the Enemy

Uncovering Lies and Choosing the Truth

How do you combat specific lies or lying feelings? First, you need to see what they are and then choose to replace them with the truth. This is a process that may take some time, especially if the lies have formed a stronghold or well-entrenched place in your thinking.

You can often find out where the lies are by making a list of what you feel or believe about a certain situation. Then, as you compare that with what you find in the Word, you can consciously choose to believe the truth instead of the lying feelings or thoughts.

For example, you may ask yourself, "How do I feel or what do I think about my situation?" Based on how you feel, you decide:

1. I'll never be any different.
2. God isn't concerned about what happens to me.
3. There is no hope.

Often just by admitting what you really feel or believe, you are able by yourself to see that they are lies. But sometimes it takes another person's objective viewpoint to see what is true and what is a lie.

From God's Word, you can see that all three of your thoughts or feelings are false. The truth for your situation is:

1. I can be different with God's help.
2. God is very concerned about what is happening to me.
3. There is hope because my God is a God of hope.

Activating Your Will

Learning to be spiritually aggressive (choosing the truth) is a process. Sometimes it is difficult to choose the truth because your will has been affected by the things you have experienced. As we have mentioned before, the feelings of helplessness that abuse victims have experienced tend to make them feel powerless. If this is true for you, you will need to reactivate your passive will.

The following affirmation may help you to reactivate your will if it has been silenced. Remember: changes happen as the will decides. You CAN choose. Read the following statement aloud. You may like to make this affirmation anytime you sense that you are feeling "weak" towards choosing what you know is true and right.

> *"I loose the enemy's hold on my will. I throw off any bindings, fogs, confusion or paralysis that he may have brought to my will. I choose to exercise my will in agreement with the truth of the Word of God. I can decide. I choose to decide. I am not helpless. I am not a victim. I am one who overwhelmingly conquers through Christ. I reactivate my will in agreement with God's choices for me."*

Daily Practice Habits

1) Meditate on the truth about what God is like by reading about Him on pages 92-104 of the "I Will Sing to the Lord" Meditation booklet found in the back of this study. One of the best ways to discover where the distortions are in your thinking is to first read over the headings of what God is like (for example: "My God is a Great God"; "My God is a Good God"; etc.).When you sense opposition inside, or thoughts to the contrary, you have a pretty good idea that that truth about God is being distorted in your mind. Mark the sections that are the hardest for you to believe and meditate on those truths.

2) Each day, read a portion of the "Truths I Believe About God" found at the end of this workout.

3) Continue to read aloud the "Daily Commitment Prayer" and the "Prayer for Restful Sleep" each day.

This Week's Spiritual Re-conditioning Record

___ Day 1 ___ Day 2 ___ Day 3 ___ Day 4

___ Day 5 ___ Day 6 ___ Day 7

Truths I Believe About God

Monday

I am important to God.
God wants to help me today.
I am not alone.

Tuesday

God is on my side.
God is always fair.
God always makes the right decisions.
God is a good and righteous judge.
God hates sin.
God spares me from His wrath because of
what Christ did on the cross for me.

Wednesday

God has realistic expectations of me today.
God accepts me.
God forgives me when I sin.
God knows when I am trying to follow
Him and He is pleased.
God really loves me.

Thursday

God suffers with me in my struggles.
God hides me in the shadow of His wings.
God has good things planned for my life.
God is concerned with meeting my physical,
spiritual and emotional needs.

Friday

God knows all the "what ifs" of my life.
God knows when I am overwhelmed.
God collects my tears. He weeps with me.
God enjoys me.
God thinks that I am precious.

Saturday

God has adopted me as His child.
God loves me with an everlasting love.
God feels compassion towards me.
God wants to bless me.
God sees everything and hears when I pray.

Sunday

God knows all about me, even my secret thoughts.
God calls me His beloved.
God chose me and brought me close to Himself.

Additional Verses For Meditation

Ps. 44:3

Rom. 8:1 & 2

Ps. 62:5-7

Ps. 55:16-18 & 22

Is. 41:10-13

Heb. 2:14-15

Ps. 69:33

Is. 44:8

John 8:36

Col. 2:15

2 Chron. 32:8

Ps. 149:6

Ps. 33:20

Ps. 59:9 & 10

Ps. 121

Lam. 3:21-25

Ps. 16:11

Is. 40:31

Ps. 38:12-15

Rom. 8:37

Ps. 71:5

Is. 49:23-25

Ps. 108:13

Ps. 46:1 & 2

Now What?

Now that you have completed the six workouts, you may like to go on to complete the following Bible study that is called "Getting to Know the Father".

Each of the six sections may be done, one a week, in any order. They can be done as an individual study, or in a group.

As we have seen, your mind is renewed by truth. These Bible studies will continue to strengthen you in the truth as they replace lies and distortions about the God you are learning to trust.

He wants to be the "Father" some have never had. Let Him be that for you.

Getting To Know The Father

Bible Study #1

Is My Heavenly Father Far Away?

Your approach to God based on the lie that He is far away would be:

> "*God, I feel like You are miles away when I try to pray to You. You seem so cold, so unemotional towards me. I try to please You, but You don't seem to understand how hard it is to follow You. When I'm afraid, it's just as though You tell me, 'Don't be silly. There's nothing to be afraid of.' You never seem to come close to me, to touch me. You don't understand how I feel. You are so stern, so serious, so distant, so unapproachable.*"

Truths from God's Word to replace the lies.

a) God sympathizes with me and with my struggles.

Heb. 4:14 & 15—

b) God wants to be intimate with me.

Matt. 1:23—

Ps. 139:3—

Ps. 63:7 & 8—

Heb. 4:16—

James 4:8—

c) Jesus shows me what God the Father is like—He is emotional.

John 11:32-38—

Matt. 9:36—

Luke 15:11-20—

d) God has good things planned for my life.

I Cor. 2:9—

Jer. 29:11-13—

e) God is concerned with meeting my physical, spiritual and emotional needs

   Ps. 138:3, 7 & 8—

   Ps. 124:1-8—

   Ps. 34:6 & 7

   Ps. 68:19 & 20—

   Additional Verses:

Getting To Know The Father

Does My Heavenly Father Really Care About Me?

Your approach to God based on the lie that He doesn't really care would be:

> "*God, I feel so alone. Do You really care? Where are You? You never seem to communicate with me. You're so busy with "important" things like running the universe, I feel like I can't, I shouldn't, bother You with the 'little' things. Besides, You aren't really that interested anyway. It's like You are in an important cosmic board meeting and don't want to be disturbed. I always feel like I'm bothering You, interrupting You. I pretend You are interested, that You care, but it doesn't help. I know You really don't.*"

Truths from God's Word to replace the lies:

a) God pays attention to me.

Ps. 34:15—

Ps. 145:18—

Eph. 2:13—

b) God cares for me.

1 Peter 5:7—

Ps. 142:5-11—

c) I am not alone.

Heb. 13:5—

Deut. 31:6—

d) God wants to help me.

Is. 9:6—

Heb. 13:6—

Ps. 20:6—

Ps. 146:5-10—

Jer. 33:3—

e) I am important to God.

Zech. 2:8—

Ps. 34:15—

Ps. 139:17 & 18—

Additional verses:

Getting To Know The Father

Will My Heavenly Father Hurt Me?

Your approach to God based on the lie that He will abuse you would be:

> *"I'm afraid of You, God. I'm afraid of Your anger. I'm afraid of Your unpredictability, afraid You will hurt me. I know I'm not worth much so I can't blame You for not loving me. But I feel nervous inside around You—on edge— like I'm waiting for You to blow up and 'get me'. My life is a mess. I wish I could trust You to help me, but I can't."*

Truths from God's Word to replace the lies:

a) God wants to help and heal me, not to hurt me.

Ps. 81:10—

Is 30:18—

Luke 12:32—

Eph. 1:3-6—

Rom. 8:32—

b) God is kind to me.

Joel 2:13—

Eph. 2:4-7—

Titus 3:4 & 5—

Jer. 9:23 & 24—

Ps. 36:7—

Jer. 31:3—

c) God is good to me.

Ps. 107:1—

Ps. 119:68—

John 10:11-15—

Ps. 86:5—

Ps. 100:1-5—

d) God has compassion for me. He treats me tenderly.

Ps. 103:13—

Ps. 111:4—

Matt. 9:36—

Mark 1:40-42—

e) I can turn to God for comfort and protection.

Is. 51:12—

2 Cor. 1:3 & 4—

Ps. 86:15-17—

John 14:16-18—

f) I can trust God when He does nice things for me.

Ps. 103:1-5—

Rom. 8:28—

1 Cor. 2:9—

Ps. 104:28—

Additional verses:

Getting To Know The Father

Can I Really Trust My Heavenly Father?

Your approach to God based on the lie that He is unreliable would be:

> "*I* guess I don't trust You, God. I know what You say, what You promise. But I'm not so sure I can count on You to do the things You have said. I can never predict how You'll feel about me from day to day. Depends on Your mood, I guess. Anyway, life has shown me that you can't count on anyone or anything, except yourself. Otherwise, you just get disappointed again. Don't expect good things to happen and then you won't be surprised when they don't."

Truths from God's Word to replace the lies:

a) God is "the Faithful One." He is totally reliable.

Heb. 10:19-23—

Phil 1:6—

Cor. 1:9—

Thess. 5:24—

Ps.145:8-21—
(Which phrases describing
God suggest that He is reliable?)

b) God is strong, unmovable, unchanging.

Ps. 91:1-4—

Ps. 125:1 & 2—

Ps. 46:7—

Heb. 13:8—

James 1:17—

Mal. 3:6—

Ps. 102:27—

Ps. 33:11—

Eccl. 7:13—

Mark 13:31—

c) It is safe for me to trust God.

Ps. 12:5—

Ps. 91:1-4—

Ps. 37:3-5—

Ps. 28:6 & 7—

1 Sam. 15:29—

Num. 23:19—

Additional verses:

Getting To Know The Father

Does My Heavenly Father Expect Too Much From Me?

Your approach to God based on the lie that He expects too much would be:

> "*God*, *my Christian life is one big endless struggle. I feel like I can never please You. I try and try but I'm never quite good enough. I feel like You have impossible expectations of me and how I should act. I feel so condemned every time I sin. You expect something from me that I can't give. You expect me to be perfect. Even when I try very hard to do the right thing, You're so critical. You seem to say, 'You can do better than that!' Every time I come to You with a problem, I seem to hear You saying, 'I don't want to hear about it!' Why bother trying? I can never live up to Your standards. Just once I'd like You to smile at me and 'hug' me and say, 'You did good enough. I am pleased with you.'"*

69

Truths from God's Word to replace the lies:

a) God has realistic expectations of me.

Ps. 103:13 & 14—

1 John 1:7-9—

.

b) Christ is my advocate with the Father. Christ is the "propitiation" for my sins. Therefore God accepts me.

1 John 2:1—

1 John 2:2—

Rom. 3:23-26—

c) God forgives me completely and totally.

   Ps. 32:1 & 2—

   Ps. 130:1-8—

d) God knows when I am trying to follow Him and He
   is pleased.

   Is. 40:11—

   John 10:3 & 4—

e) God is more concerned about my heart than with my accomplishments.

    2 Cor. 3:5 & 6—

    1 Sam. 16:6 & 7—

f) God really loves me.

    Jer. 31:3—

    Eph. 2:4—

    1 John 4:10 & 19—

Rom. 8:38 & 39—

Additional verses:

Getting To Know The Father

Will My Heavenly Father Leave Me?

Your approach to God based on the lie that He will abandon you would be:

> "*God*, I know that sooner or later, You'll get tired of putting up with me and You'll pull away. I'd probably deserve it. I sense a desperate drive to please You, to be good, so You won't reject me. But I'm always so afraid You will. It all seems to be up to me, and I know how I usually mess things up. I feel like I'm adrift in a rowboat with no oars, and the bottom is a long way off!"

Truths from God's Word to replace the lies:

a) God considers me to be valuable and "worth sticking with".

Ps. 149:4—

Ps. 37: 23 & 24—

Ps. 18:19—

Matt. 10:29-31—

Matt. 12:10-12—

b) God does not lie. He will not hurt me. I can trust
   Him when He is good to me.

   Num. 23:19—

John 3:33—

Ps. 118:6—

Ps. 56:9—

Rom. 8:31—

c) God is my security. He will not abandon me.

Ps. 91:14-16—

Ps. 18:35—

Heb. 13:5—

d) God takes the initiative in seeking a relationship
with me.

Eph. 2:1-9—

Luke 15:3-6—

e) God lasts forever.

Deut. 33:27—

Ps. 90:2—

Jer. 31:3—

f) God wants me to come to Him with everything.
1 Peter 5:7—

Luke 21:34—

Additional verses:

Bible Study #7

True Security !!

Being secure in Christ and *feeling* secure in Christ may be two different things. Even if you don't "feel" or "really believe" that the following statements about God are true, choose to believe them. They are true! As you persist in agreeing with the truth, the feelings of security in Christ will grow and bear fruit in your actions.

This I Know: **God Is Always Paying Attention To Me!**

Gen. 16:13—

Ps. 17:8—

Ps. 32:8—

Ps. 33:18—

Ps. 101:6—

Ps. 139:16—

This I Know: **God Hears Me And Wants To Help Me!**

Ps. 4:3—

Ps. 34:6 & 17—

Ps. 40:1-3—

Ps. 55:17—

Ps. 116:1—

Ps. 61:2—

Ps. 124:2-4—

This I Know: **God Is Near Me!**

Ps. 119:151—

Ps. 34:18—

Is. 50:8—

Ps. 139:7-12—

Ps. 16:11—

Additional Verses:

I Will Sing to the Lord

"I will sing to the Lord as long as I live; I will sing praise to my God while I have my being. Let my meditation be pleasing to Him; As for me, I shall be glad in the Lord"

(Ps. 104:33 & 34)

Verses for Meditation

"Set Your Mind"....

Meditate by Exalting Him From His Word

"*W*orthy is the Lamb that was slain to receive power and riches and wisdom and might and honor and glory and blessing.... To Him who sits on the throne, and to the Lamb, be blessing and honor and glory and dominion forever and ever....Amen."

(Rev.5:12 & 13)

"*P*raise the Lord! Praise,O servants of the Lord. Praise the name of the Lord. Blessed be the name of the Lord from this time forth and forever. From the rising of the sun to its setting the name of the Lord is to be praised. The Lord is high above all nations; His glory is above the heavens. Who is like the Lord our God, who is enthroned on high, who humbles Himself to behold the things that are in heaven and in the earth?...Praise the Lord!"

(Ps. 113:1-9)

"*H*OLY, HOLY, HOLY is the Lord God, the Almighty, who was and who is and who is to come."

(Rev. 4:8)

"*I* will bless the Lord at all times; His praise shall continually be in my mouth. My soul shall make its boast in the Lord; The humble shall hear it and rejoice. O magnify the Lord with me, and let us exalt His name together."

(Ps. 34:1-3)

"*W*orthy art Thou, our Lord and our God, to receive glory and honor and power; for Thou didst create all things, and because of Thy will they existed, and were created."

(Rev. 4:11)

"*W*orthy art Thou to take the book and to break its seals; for Thou wast slain, and didst purchase for God with Thy blood men from every tribe and tongue and people and nation. And Thou hast made them to be a kingdom and priests to our God; and they shall reign upon the earth."

(Rev. 5:9 & 10)

"*G*reat and marvelous are Thy works, O Lord God, the Almighty; Righteous and true are Thy ways, Thou King of the nations. Who will not fear, O Lord, and glorify Thy name? For Thou alone art HOLY; For all the nations will come and worship before Thee, for Thy righteous acts have been revealed."

(Rev. 15: 3 & 4)

"*O* God, Thou art my God; I shall seek Thee earnestly; My soul thirsts for Thee, my flesh yearns for Thee, in a dry and weary land where there is no water. Thus I have beheld Thee in the sanctuary, to see Thy power and Thy glory. Because Thy lovingkindness is better than life, my lips will praise Thee. So I will bless Thee as long as I live;

I will lift up my hands in Thy name. My soul is satisfied as with marrow and fatness, and my mouth offers praises with joyful lips. When I remember Thee on my bed, I meditate on Thee in the night watches. For Thou hast been my help, and in the shadow of Thy wings I sing for joy. My soul clings to Thee, Thy right hand upholds me."

(Ps. 63:1-8)

"Now to the King eternal, immortal, invisible, the only God, be honor and glory forever and ever. Amen."

(I Tim. 1:17)

"The Lord reigns. He is clothed with majesty; The Lord has clothed and girded Himself with strength; Indeed the world is firmly established, it will not be moved. Thy Throne is established from of old; Thou art from everlasting."

(Ps. 93:1 & 2)

"He who is the blessed and only Sovereign, the King of Kings and the Lord of Lords; who alone possesses immortality and dwells in unapproachable lights. Whom no man has seen or can see. To Him be honor and eternal dominion! AMEN."

(I Tim. 6:15 & 16)

"*I* will extol Thee, my God, O King; and I will bless Thy name forever and ever! Every day I will bless Thee, and I will praise Thy name forever and ever. Great is the Lord, and highly to be praised; And His greatness is unsearchable! One generation shall praise Thy works to another, and shall declare Thy mighty acts. On the glorious splendor of Thy majesty, and on Thy wonderful works I will meditate. And men shall speak of the power of Thine awesome acts; And I will tell of Thy greatness. They shall eagerly utter (bubble over) with the memory of Thine abundant goodness, and shall shout joyfully of Thy righteousness."

(Ps. 145:1-7)

"*B*lessed be the Lord God, the God of Israel, who alone works wonders. And blessed be His glorious name forever; And may the whole earth be filled with His glory. Amen, and amen."

(Ps. 72:18)

Other verses:

Focus on the Lord by Confessing His Name

"*T*hrough Him, then, let us continually offer up a sacrifice of praise to God, that is, the fruit of lips that give thanks(confess) His name."

(Heb. 13:15)

"*T*herefore also God highly exalted Him, and bestowed on Him the name which is above every name, that at the name of Jesus every knee should bow, of those who are in heaven, and on earth, and under the earth, and that every tongue should confess that Jesus Christ is Lord, to the glory of God the Father."

(Phil. 2:9-11)

THE LORD JESUS CHRIST.......
　　　　　　the name above every name.

THE LORD JESUS CHRIST.......
　　　　　　image of the invisible God.

THE LORD JESUS CHRIST.......
　　　　　　head over all rule and authority.

THE LORD JESUS CHRIST.......
　　　　　　mediator between God and man.

THE LORD JESUS CHRIST.......
　　　　　　the exact representation of God's being

THE LORD JESUS CHRIST.......
            author of our salvation.

THE LORD JESUS CHRIST.......
            the lion of the tribe of Judah.

THE LORD JESUS CHRIST.......
            the Lamb that was slain.

THE LORD JESUS CHRIST......
            the source of eternal salvation.

THE LORD JESUS CHRIST.......
            the Great Shepherd.

THE LORD JESUS CHRIST.......
            our Advocate with the Father.

THE LORD JESUS CHRIST.......
            God's Beloved Son.

THE LORD JESUS CHRIST.......
            the Messiah.

THE LORD JESUS CHRIST.......
            Immanuel, God with us.

THE LORD JESUS CHRIST.......
            a Savior, who is Christ the Lord.

THE LORD JESUS CHRIST.......
            the Prince of life.

THE LORD JESUS CHRIST.......
> judge of the living and the dead.

THE LORD JESUS CHRIST.......
> the power of God.

THE LORD JESUS CHRIST.......
> our righteousness.

THE LORD JESUS CHRIST.......
> our master in heaven.

THE LORD JESUS CHRIST.......
> heir of all things.

THE LORD JESUS CHRIST.......
> a merciful and faithful High Priest.

THE LORD JESUS CHRIST.......
> the author and perfecter of faith.

THE LORD JESUS CHRIST........
> the Alpha and Omega.

THE LORD JESUS CHRIST.......
> the Word of God.

THE LORD JESUS CHRIST........
> our life.

THE LORD JESUS CHRIST.......
> our Passover.

THE LORD JESUS CHRIST.......
                    King of Kings and Lord of Lords.

THE LORD JESUS CHRIST........
                    My Lord and My God!

Meditate on what He is like

My God is a Great God

"*O* come, let us sing for joy to the Lord; Let us shout joyfully to the rock of our salvation. Let us come before His presence with thanksgiving; Let us shout joyfully to Him with psalms. For the Lord is a great God, and a great King above all gods. In whose hand are the depths of the earth; The peaks of the mountains are His also. The sea is His, for it was He who made it; And His hands formed the dry land. Come, let us worship and bow down; Let us kneel before the Lord our Maker. For He is our God, and we are the people of his pasture, and the sheep of His hand; . . .For I know that the Lord is great, and that our Lord is above all gods. Whatever the Lord pleases, He does, in heaven and in earth, in the sea and in all deeps; . . .There is no one like Thee among the gods, O Lord; nor are there any works like Thine. All nations whom Thou hast made shall come and worship before Thee, O Lord; And they shall glorify Thy name. For Thou art great and doest wondrous deeds; Thou alone art God."

(Ps. 95:1-7; Ps. 135:5-6; Ps. 86:8-10)

My God Reigns

"*He* who is the blessed and only Sovereign, the King of kings and Lord of Lords; . . .Thy throne, O God, is forever and ever; A scepter of uprightness is the scepter of Thy kingdom; . . .The Lord reigns. He is clothed with majesty; The Lord has clothed and girded Himself with strength; Indeed, the world is firmly established, it will not be moved. Thy throne is established from of old; Thou are from everlasting."

(I Tim.6:15; Ps, 45:6; Ps.93:2)

'The Lord has established His throne in the heavens; And His sovereignty rules over all. Bless the Lord, you His angels, mighty in strength, who perform His word, obeying the voice of His word! Bless the Lord, all you His hosts, you who serve Him, doing His will. Bless the Lord, all you works of His, in all places of His dominion; Bless the Lord, O my soul!"

(Ps. 103:19-22)

My God is a Good God

"O taste and see that the Lord is good; How blessed is the man who takes refuge in Him! . . .How great is Thy goodness, which Thou hast stored up for those who fear Thee, which Thou hast wrought for those who take refuge in Thee; . . .Shout joyfully to the Lord, all the earth. Serve the Lord with gladness; Come before Him with joyful singing. Know that the Lord Himself is God; It is He who has made us, and not we ourselves; We are Him people and the sheep of His pasture. Enter His gates with thanksgiving, and His courts with praise. Give thanks to Him; Bless His name. For the Lord is good; His lovingkindness is everlasting, and His faithfulness to all generations."

(Ps. 34:8; Ps. 31:19; Ps. 100:1-5)

My God is a Holy God

"*Who* is like Thee among the gods, O Lord? Who is like Thee, majestic in holiness; . . .In the year of King Uzziah's death, I saw the Lord, sitting on a throne, lofty and exalted, with the train of His robe filling the temple. Seraphim stood above Him, each having six wings...and one called out to another and said, 'Holy, holy, holy, is the Lord of hosts, the whole earth is full of His glory;' . . .The Lord reigns, let the peoples tremble; He is enthroned above the cherubim, let the earth shake! The Lord is great in Zion, and He is exalted above the peoples. Let them praise Thy great and awesome name; Holy is He. And the strength of the King loves justice; Thou hast established equity; Thou hast executed justice and right-eousness in Jacob. Exalt the Lord our God, and worship at His footstool; Holy is He."

(Ex. 15:11; Is. 6:1-3; Ps. 99:1-5)

My God is a Just God

"*I* proclaim the name of the Lord; Ascribe greatness to our God! The Rock! His work is perfect, for all His ways are just; A God of faithfulness and without injustice, right-eous and upright is He; . . .For Christ also died for sins once for all, the just for the unjust, in order that He might bring us to God."

(Deut. 32:3 & 4; I Peter 3:18)

94

My God is a Loving God

"*P*raise the Lord! Oh, give thanks to the Lord, for He is good; for His lovingkindness is everlasting."

(Ps. 106:1)

"*T*he Lord appeared to him(me) from afar, saying, 'I have loved you with an everlasting love; Therefore I have drawn you with lovingkindness.'"

(Jer. 31:3)

"*B*y this the love of God was manifested in us, that God has sent His only begotten Son into the world so that we might live through Him. In this is love, not that we loved God, but that He loved us and sent His Son to be the propitiation for our sins."

(I John 4:9 & 10)

"*F*or I am convinced that neither death, nor life, nor angels, nor principalities, nor things present, nor things to come, nor powers, nor height, nor depth, nor any other created thing, shall be able to separate us from the love of God, which is in Christ Jesus our Lord."

(Rom. 8:38 & 39)

My God is a Mighty God

"*T*o the only wise God, through Jesus Christ, to whom be the glory forever. Amen; . . .There is none like Thee, O Lord; Thou are great, and great is Thy name in might.

Who would not fear Thee, O King of the nations? Indeed it is Thy due! For among all the wise men of the nations, and in all their kingdoms, there is none like Thee."

(Rom. 16:27; Jer. 10:6-7; Col. 2:3)

"*I* am God Almighty(El Shaddai)."

(Gen. 17:1)

"*The* Lord appeared to him(me) from afar, saying, 'I have loved you with an everlasting love; Therefore I have drawn you with lovingkindness.'"

(Jer. 31:3)

"*By* this the love of God was manifested in us, that God has sent His only begotten Son into the world so that we might live through Him. In this is love, not that we loved God, but that He loved us and sent His Son to be the propitiation for our sins."

(I John 4:9 & 10)

"*For* I am convinced that neither death, nor life, nor angels, nor principalities, nor things present, nor things to come, nor powers, nor height, nor depth, nor any other created thing, shall be able to separate us from the love of God, which is in Christ Jesus our Lord."

(Rom. 8:38-39)

My God is a Wise God

"*To* the only wise God, through Jesus Christ, to whom be the glory forever. Amen; . . .There is none like Thee, O Lord; Thou are great, and great is Thy name in might. Who would not fear Thee, O King of the nations? Indeed it is Thy due! For among all the wise men of the nations, and in all their kingdoms, there is none like Thee; . . .Christ ...in whom are hidden all the treasures of wisdom and knowledge."

(Rom. 16:27; Jer. 10:6-7; Col. 2:3)

"*S*ing to God, O kingdoms of the earth; Sing praises to the Lord. Selah. To Him who rides upon the highest heavens, which are from ancient times; Behold, He speaks forth with His voice, a mighty voice. Ascribe strength to God; His majesty is over Israel, and His strength is in the skies. O God, Thou are awesome from Thy sanctuary. The God of Israel gives strength and power to the people. Blessed be God!"

(Ps. 68:32-35)

"*B*lessed are Thou, O Lord God of Israel our father, forever and ever. Thine O Lord is the greatness and the power and the glory and the victory and the majesty, indeed everything that is in the heavens and the earth; Thine is the dominion, O Lord, and Thou dost exalt Thyself as head over all. Both riches and honor come from Thee, and Thou dost rule over all, and in Thy hand is power and might; and it lies in Thy hand to make great, and to strengthen everyone. Now therefore our God, we thank Thee, and praise Thy glorious name."

(I Chron. 29:10-13)

My God is a Compassionate God

"The Lord is compassionate and gracious, slow to anger and abounding in lovingkindness...Just as a father has compassion on his children, so the Lord has compassion on those who fear (revere) Him."

(Ps. 103:8 & 13)

"And Jesus was going about all the cities and the villages, teaching in their synagogues, and proclaiming the gospel of the kingdom, and healing every kind of disease and every kind of sickness. And seeing the multitudes, He felt compassion for them, because they were distressed and downcast like sheep without a shepherd."

(Matt. 9:35-36)

"Therefore, when Mary came where Jesus was, she saw Him and fell at His feet, saying to Him, 'Lord, if You had been here, my brother would not have died.' When Jesus therefore saw her weeping, and the Jews who came with her, also weeping, He was deeply moved in spirit, and was troubled, and said, 'Where have you laid him?' They said to Him, 'Lord, come and see.' Jesus wept. And so the Jews were saying, 'Behold how He loved him!' "

(John 11:32-36)

My God is a God of Truth

"*A*nd the Word became flesh, and dwelt among us, and we beheld His glory, glory as of the only begotten from the Father, full of grace and truth; . . . Jesus said to him, 'I am the way, and the truth, and the life; no one comes to the Father, but through Me.'"

(John 1:14; John 14:6)

My God is Everywhere

"*H*eaven is My throne, and the earth is My footstool."

(Is. 66:1)

"(*T*here is)...one God and Father of all who is over all and through all and in all."

(Eph. 4:6)

"*W*here can I go from Thy Spirit? Or where can I flee from Thy presence? If I ascend to heaven, Thou art there; If I make my bed in Sheol, behold, Thou art there. If I take the wings of the dawn, if I dwell in the remotest part of the sea, even there Thy hand will lead me, and Thy right hand will lay hold of me."

(Ps. 139:7-10)

My God is a Triune God

"*B*lessed be the God and Father of our Lord Jesus

Christ who has blessed us with every spiritual blessing in the heavenly places in Christ . . .He predestined us to adoption as sons through Jesus Christ to Himself...having also believed, you were sealed in Him with the Holy Spirit of promise."

(Eph. 1:3,5 & 13)

"*The* grace of the Lord Jesus Christ, and the love of God, and the fellowship of the Holy Spirit, be with you all."

(2 Cor. 13:14)

My God is a Merciful and Gracious God

"*But* God, being rich in mercy, because of His great love with which He loved us, even when we were dead in our transgressions, made us alive together with Christ (by grace you have been saved) and raised us up with Him, and seated us with Him in the heavenly places, in Christ Jesus, in order that in the ages to come He might show the surpassing riches of His grace in kindness toward us in Christ Jesus."

(Eph. 2:4-7)

"*The* Lord is gracious and merciful; Slow to anger and great in lovingkindness. The Lord is good to all, and His mercies are over all His works."

(Ps. 145:8 & 9)

My God is an Eternal God

"*F*or a child will be born to us, a son will be given to us; And the government will rest on His shoulders; And His name will be called Wonderful Counselor, Mighty God, Eternal Father, Prince of Peace..."

(Is. 9:6)

"*B*efore the mountains were born, or Thou didst give birth to the earth and the world, even from everlasting to everlasting, Thou are God; . . .Trust in the Lord forever, for in God the Lord, we have an everlasting Rock;...His dominion is an everlasting dominion, and His kingdom endures from generation to generation;...The eternal God is a dwelling place, and underneath are the everlasting arms."

(Ps. 90:2; Is. 26:4; Dan. 4:34; Deut. 33:27)

My God is a Righteous God

"*T*he Lord is righteous in all His ways, and kind in all His deeds;...Righteous art Thou, O Lord, and upright are Thy judgements; . . .Righteousness and justice are the foundation of Thy throne; Lovingkindness and truth go before Thee; . . .We have an Advocate with the Father, Jesus Christ, the righteous."

(Ps. 145:17; Ps. 119:137; Ps. 89:14; I John 2:1)

My God is a Forgiving God

"*F*or Thou, Lord, art good, and ready to forgive, and abundant in lovingkindness to all who call upon Thee; . . .He is faithful and righteous to forgive us our sins and to cleanse us; . . .If Thou, Lord, shouldst mark iniquities, O Lord, who could stand? But there is forgiveness with Thee, that Thou mayest be feared."

(Ps. 86:5; I John 1:9; Ps. 130:3 & 4)

My God is a Kind God

"*G*ive thanks to the Lord, for He is good; For His lovingkindness is everlasting. Give thanks to the God of gods, for His lovingkindness is everlasting. Give thanks to the Lord of lords, for His lovingkindness is everlasting; To Him who alone does great wonders, for His lovingkindness is everlasting; . . .Who remembered us in our low estate, for His lovingkindness is everlasting, and has rescued us from our adversaries, for his lovingkindness is everlasting; Who gives food to all flesh, for His lovingkindness is everlasting. Give thanks to the God of heaven, for His lovingkindness is everlasting; . . .He has not dealt with us according to our sins, nor rewarded us according to our iniquities. For high as the heavens are above the earth, so great is His lovingkindness toward those who fear(revere) Him. As far as the east is from the west, so far has He removed our transgressions from us."

(Ps. 136:1-4, 23-26; Ps. 103:10-11)

My God is a Faithful God

"*T*he heavens will praise Thy wonders, O Lord, Thy faithfulness also in the assembly of the holy ones. For who in the skies is comparable to the Lord? Who among the sons of the mighty is like the Lord, a God greatly feared in the council of the holy ones, and awesome above all those who are around Him? O Lord God of hosts, who is like Thee, O mighty Lord? Thy faithfulness also surrounds Thee; . . .This I recall to my mind, therefore I have hope. The Lord's lovingkindnesses indeed never cease, for His compassions never fail. They are new every morning; Great is Thy faithfulness."

(Ps. 89:5-8; Lam. 3:21-23)

My God Knows Everything

"Great is our Lord, and abundant in strength;   His understanding is infinite; . . .O Lord, Thou hast searched me and known me. Thou dost know when I sit down and when I rise up; Thou dost understand my thoughts from afar. Thou dost scrutinize my path and my lying down, and art intimately acquainted with all my ways. Even before there is a word on my tongue, behold, O Lord, Thou dost know it all; . . .There is no creature hidden form His sight, but all things are open and laid bare to the eyes of Him with whom we have to do: . . .He knows the way I take."

(Ps. 147:5; 139:1-4; Heb.4:13; Job 23:10)

My God Never Changes

"... I the Lord, do not change..."

(Malachi 3:6)

"*Jesus* Christ is the same yesterday and today, yes and forever."

(Heb. 13:8)

"*Every* good thing bestowed and every perfect gift is from above, coming down from the Father of lights, with whom there is no variation, or shifting shadow."

(James 1:17)

"*Forever*, O Lord, Thy word is settled (stands firm) in heaven."

(Ps. 119:89)

Other verses:

Focus on the Cross

"And the soldiers took Him away into the palace (that is the Praetorium), and they called together the whole Roman cohort. And they dressed Him up in purple, and after weaving a crown of thorns, they put it on Him; and they began to acclaim Him, 'Hail, King of the Jews!' And they kept beating His head with a reed, and spitting at Him, and kneeling and bowing before Him. And after they had mocked Him, they took the purple off Him, and put His garments on Him. And they led Him out to crucify Him...And they brought Him to the place Golgotha, which is translated, Place of a Skull. And they tried to give Him wine mixed with myrrh; but He did not take it. And they crucified Him, and dividing up His garments among themselves, casting lots for them, to decide what each should take. And it was the third hour (9 am) when they crucified Him. And the inscription of the charge against Him read, 'THE KING OF THE JEWS.' . . .And when the sixth hour (noon) had come, darkness fell over the whole land until the ninth hour (3pm). And at the ninth hour Jesus cried out with a loud voice, 'Eloi, Eloi, Lama Sabachthani?' which is translated, 'My God, My God, why hast Thou forsaken Me?' . . .And Jesus, crying out with a loud voice, said, 'Father, into Thy hands I commit My Spirit.' And having said this, He breathed His last . . .And the veil of the temple was torn in two from top to bottom."

(Mark 15:16-20, 22-26, 33-34; Luke 23:46; Mark 15;38)

"And Joseph brought a linen sheet, took Him down, wrapped Him in the linen sheet, and laid Him in a tomb which had been hewn out in the rock; and he rolled a stone against the entrance of the tomb; . . .But on the first day of the week, at early dawn, they came to the tomb, bringing the spices which they had prepared. And they found the stone rolled away from the tomb, but when they entered, they did not find the body of the Lord Jesus. And it happened that while they were perplexed about this, behold, two men suddenly stood near them in dazzling apparel; and as the women were terrified and bowed their faces to the ground, the men said to them, 'Why do you seek the living One among the dead? He is not here, but He has risen. Remember how He spoke to you, while He was still in Galilee, saying that the Son of Man must be delivered into the hands of sinful men, and be crucified, and the third day rise again.'"

(Mark 15:46; Luke 24:1-7)

"*A*nd He Himself bore our sins in His body on the cross, that we might die to sin and live to righteousness; for by His wounds you were healed."

(I Pet. 2:24)

"*S*urely our griefs He Himself bore, and our sorrows He carried; Yet we ourselves esteemed Him stricken, smitten of God, and afflicted. But He was pierced through for our transgressions, He was crushed for our iniquities; The chastening for our well-being fell upon Him, and by His scourging we are healed. All of us like sheep have gone astray, each of us has turned to his own way; But the Lord has caused the iniquity of us all to fall on Him."

(Is. 53:4-6)

"Since then the children share in flesh and blood, He Himself likewise also partook of the same, that through death He might render powerless him who had the power of death, that is, the devil; and might deliver those who through fear of death were subject to slavery all their lives."

(Heb. 2:14 & 15)

"But when Christ appeared as a high priest. . .He entered. . . the . . .tabernacle . . .not through the blood of goats and calves, but through His own blood, He entered the holy place once for all, having obtained eternal redemption. For if the blood of goats and bulls. . . sanctify for the cleansing of the flesh, how much more will the blood of Christ, who through the eternal Spirit offered Himself without blemish to God, cleanse your conscience from dead works to serve the living God?"

(Heb. 9:11-14)

"And when you were dead in your transgressions and the uncircumcision of your flesh, He made you alive together with Him, having forgiven us all our transgressions, having cancelled out the certificate of debt consisting of decrees against us and which was hostile to us; and He has taken it out of the way, having nailed it to the cross."

(Col. 2:13 & 14)

"For He delivered us from the domain of darkness, and transferred us to the kingdom of His beloved Son, in whom we have redemption, the forgiveness of sins."

(Col. 1:13 & 14)

"*But* may it never be that I should boast, except in the cross of our Lord Jesus Christ, through which the world has been crucified to me, and I to the world."

(Gal. 6:14)

Meditate on the Incomparable Christ

"*He* is the image of the invisible God, the first-born of all creation. For in Him all things were created, both in the heavens and on earth, visible and invisible, whether thrones or dominions or rulers or authorities—all things have been created through Him and for Him. And He is before all things, and in Him all things hold together. He is also head of the body, the church; and He Himself is the beginning, the first-born from the dead; so that He might come to have first place in everything. For it was the Father's good pleasure for all the fullness to dwell in Him; and through Him to reconcile all things to Himself, having made peace through the blood of His cross."

(Col. 1:15-20)

"*And* I turned to see the voice that was speaking with me. And having turned, I saw seven golden lampstands; and in the middle of the lampstands one like a son of man, clothed in a robe reaching to the feet, and girded across His breast with a golden girdle. And His head and His hair were white like white wool, like snow; and His eyes were like a flame of fire; and His feet were like burnished bronze, when it has been caused to glow in a furnace, and His voice was like the sound of many waters. And in His right hand He held seven stars; and out of His mouth came a sharp two-edged sword; and His face was like the sun shining in its strength. And when I saw Him, I fell at His feet as a dead man. And He laid His right hand upon me, saying, 'Do not be afraid; I am the first and the last, and the living One; and I was dead, and behold, I am alive forever more, and I have the keys of death and of Hades.'"

(Rev. 1:12-18)

"*G*od, after He spoke long ago to the fathers in the prophets in many portions and in many ways, in these last days has spoken to us in His Son, whom He appointed heir of all things, through whom also He made the world. And He is the radiance of His glory and the exact representation of His nature, and upholds all things by the word of His power. When He had made purification of sins, He sat down at the right hand of the Majesty on high."

(Heb. 1:1-3)

"*A*nd I saw heaven opened; and behold, a white horse, and He who sat upon it is called Faithful and True; and in righteousness He judges and wages war. And His eyes are a flame of fire, and upon His head are many diadems; and He has a name written upon Him which no one knows except Himself. And He is clothed with a robe dipped in blood; and His name is called The Word of God. And the armies which are in heaven, clothed in fine linens, white and clean, were following Him on white horses. And from His mouth comes a sharp sword, so that with it He may smite the nations; and He will rule them with a rod of iron; and He treads the wine press of the fierce wrath of God, the Almighty. And on His robe and on His thigh He has a name written, 'KING OF KINGS, AND LORD OF LORDS!' "

(Rev. 19:11-16)

Look Forward to His Return

"*If* we believe that Jesus died and rose again, even so God will bring with Him those who have fallen asleep in Jesus. For this we say to you by the word of the Lord, that we who are alive, and remain until the coming of the Lord, shall not precede those who have fallen asleep. For the Lord Himself will descend from heaven with a shout, with the voice of the archangel, and with the trumpet of God; and the dead in Christ shall rise first. Then we who are alive and remain shall be caught up together with them in the clouds to meet the Lord in the air, and thus we shall always be with the Lord."

(I Thess. 4: 14-17)

"*You* too be patient; strengthen your hearts, for the coming of the Lord is at hand."

(James 5: 8)

"*In* the same way (He took) the cup also, after supper, saying 'This cup is the new covenant in My blood; do this, as often as you drink it, in remembrance of Me. For as often as you eat this bread and drink the cup, you proclaim the Lord's death until He comes.' "

(I Cor. 11: 25-26)

"*Let* not your heart be troubled; (you) believe in God believe also in Me. In My Father's house are many dwelling places; if it were not so, I would have told you; for I go to prepare a place for you. And if I go and prepare a place for you, I will come again, and receive you to Myself; that where I am, there you may be also."

(John 14:1-3)

"*But* the day of the Lord will come like a thief, in which the heavens will pass away with a roar and the elements will be destroyed with intense heat, and the earth and its works will be burned up. Since all these things are to be destroyed in this way, what sort of people ought you to be in holy conduct and godliness, looking for and hastening the coming of the day of God, on account of which the heavens will be destroyed by burning, and the elements will melt with intense heat. But according to His promise we are looking for new heavens and a new earth, in which righteousness dwells. Therefore, beloved, since you look for these things, be diligent to be found by Him in peace, spotless and blameless."

(2 Pet. 3: 10-14)

"*The* Spirit and the bride say, 'Come.' And let the one who hears say, 'Come.' . . .He who testifies to these things say, 'Yes, I am coming quickly.' Amen. Come, Lord Jesus."

(Rev. 22: 17-20)

Notes

Notes

Notes

Notes